The Navajo

**KEVIN CUNNINGHAM
AND PETER BENOIT**

Children's Press®
An Imprint of Scholastic Inc.
New York Toronto London Auckland Sydney
Mexico City New Delhi Hong Kong
Danbury, Connecticut

Content Consultant
Scott Manning Stevens, PhD
Director, McNickle Center
Newberry Library
Chicago, Illinois

Library of Congress Cataloging-in-Publication Data

Cunningham, Kevin, 1966–
  The Navajo/Kevin Cunningham and Peter Benoit.
     p. cm. — (A true book)
  Includes bibliographical references and index.
  ISBN-13: 978-0-531-20762-8 (lib. bdg.)   ISBN 978-0-531-29304-1 (pbk.)
  ISBN-10: 0-531-20762-5 (lib. bdg.)   0-531-29304-1 (pbk.)
  1. Navajo Indians—Juvenile literature. 2. Indians of North America—Southwest, New. I. Benoit,
Peter, 1955– II. Title.
  E99.N3C865 2011
  979.1004'9726—dc22   2010050837

All rights reserved. Published in 2011 by Children's Press, an imprint of Scholastic Inc.
Printed in China 62
SCHOLASTIC, CHILDREN'S PRESS, A TRUE BOOK and associated logos are trademarks and/or
registered trademarks of Scholastic Inc.

3 4 5 6 7 8 9 10 R 19 18 17 16 15 14 13 12

Find the Truth!

Everything you are about to read is true *except* for one of the sentences on this page.

Which one is **TRUE**?

T or F In the 1930s, the U.S. government killed more than four-fifths of the livestock on Navajo lands.

T or F Kachina dolls are sacred objects to the Navajo.

Find the answers in this book.

3

Contents

1 Where It All Began

Where did the Navajo come from?............ 7

2 The Age of Raiding and Trading

How did the Navajo get along with the
Spaniards and with other tribes?............ 13

3 The Navajo's Conflicts

How did the U.S. government react to
Navajo raids?.............................. 21

THE **BIG** TRUTH!

Land of Suffering

What did the Navajo experience
on the Long Walk? 26

Navajo rider

Navajo necklace

4 The Navajo Nation

What is life like in Dinétah in modern
times? 29

5 Navajo Culture

What are some **traditional** Navajo
beliefs and crafts? 37

True Statistics 43

Resources 44

Important Words 46

Index 47

About the Authors 48

Navajo homes were made with natural materials that helped them stay cool in the summer and warm in the winter.

Hogan

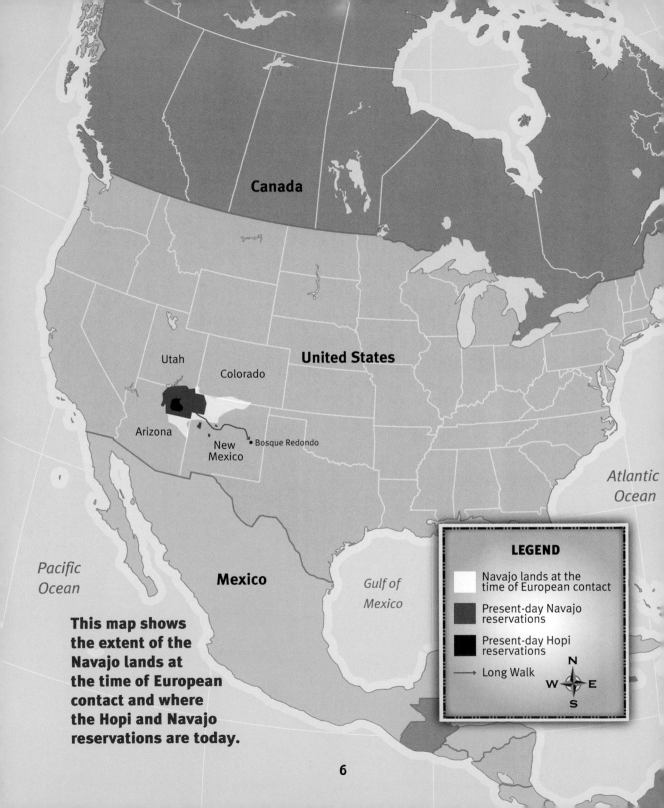

Canada

United States

Utah

Colorado

Arizona

New
Mexico

• Bosque Redondo

Atlantic
Ocean

Pacific
Ocean

Mexico

Gulf of
Mexico

**This map shows
the extent of the
Navajo lands at
the time of European
contact and where
the Hopi and Navajo
reservations are today.**

LEGEND

Navajo lands at the
time of European contact

Present-day Navajo
reservations

Present-day Hopi
reservations

→ Long Walk

N
W   E
S

CHAPTER 1

Where It All Began

A thousand or more years ago, the ancestors of the Navajo people lived near Great Slave Lake in northwestern Canada. They called themselves the Diné (meaning "the people"). They spoke an **Athabascan** language related to languages still spoken by native peoples such as the Denesuline and the Slavey, who live in today's Canada and Alaska. By the 1200s, large numbers of Diné had **migrated** to the American Southwest.

Today, more than 170,000 Navajo speak Diné Bizaad, the traditional Navajo language.

Adopting New Ways

In the Southwest, the Diné at first lived as they long had—by gathering wild plants and hunting animals for meat. Throughout Navajo history, the Diné often adopted other peoples' good ideas. In the 1200s, for example, they began to trade goods with southwestern Pueblo peoples such as the Hopi and the Zuni. While these native groups had been actively trading, the Navajo had focused more on hunting and gathering.

A Pueblo woman decorates pottery. The Navajo learned to make pottery from the Pueblo.

Not all corn is yellow. The Pueblo raised red and blue corn, too.

A Pueblo farmer tends a corn plant. Some farming tools had long handles, with blades made from animal bones.

The Pueblo peoples lived as farmers. They could trade Diné hunters new foods and fabrics in return for bison (buffalo) meat and hides. Though the desert Southwest offered little water, the Pueblo channeled it with ditches and held it in man-made lakes. That allowed them to grow squash, beans, and the most important crop of all, maize (corn). They also wove and traded cotton, a plant fiber good for making clothes and other things.

The Four Corners region is home to Monument Valley. Over many years, wind and other natural forces shaped the rock formations found in the area.

Dinétah

The Diné lived in an area they call Dinétah (dee-NEH-tah), in what is known today as the Four Corners region. This region includes parts of modern-day Colorado, New Mexico, Arizona, and Utah. The Navajo's story of the world's creation takes place in Dinétah. They consider it a holy place. Much of Dinétah stands a mile or more above sea level. Flat-topped **mesas** rise over the landscape. The San Juan River runs near a maze of canyons.

Though Dinétah has no borders, the center of it sits within an area surrounded by Hesperus Peak to the north, Blanca Peak to the east, Mount Taylor to the south, and the San Francisco Peaks to the west. By 1500, the Diné had made the area their own. It was only around 1750 that other groups of people began to push them to move. One group came from across the Atlantic Ocean—the Spanish.

The Navajo name for Hesperus Peak means "big mountain sheep."

The Spanish enter a
Pueblo settlement
called Hawikuh.

CHAPTER 2

The Age of Raiding and Trading

The Spanish conquered central Mexico in the 1500s. Over the next century, they worked their way north. Eventually they built settlements east of Dinétah and named the nearby Diné the Navajo. The Spanish also pushed into Pueblo lands and mistreated them. Mine owners made them dig for minerals. Priests prevented them from practicing their religions and ordered them to worship in Catholic churches.

Some Spanish soldiers wore heavy meal armor in the hot American Southwest.

The Spanish introduced cattle to the Pueblo. Some raiding native groups stole cattle from Pueblo villages.

Native groups banded together to push back the Spaniards. At the same time, the Navajo and another Athabascan-language people, the Apache, **raided** the Pueblo peoples who helped the Spanish. The Spanish answered by building forts and sending in soldiers to protect themselves and their allies, the Pueblos. But the Spanish had already brought something that would make the Navajo tougher and harder to catch.

Horse People

Before 1492, no horses lived in North or South America. The wild horses that once roamed both continents had died out at the end of the last Ice Age. But there were still horses in Europe. As Europeans began to settle the Americas, they brought horses along to help in war, farming, and exploration. Native peoples were impressed by the animals. Once Spanish settlers brought horses north, the Navajo's lives changed.

The Navajo learned to ride horses by the early 1600s.

Horses made travel faster and easier for the Navajo.

The Pueblo battle the Spanish in 1680.

The horse allowed the Navajo and their Apache allies to make quick raids. When **drought** struck in the 1670s, they ignored the Spanish soldiers and raided Pueblo peoples for food. The Pueblos were angry about the raids and the lack of support from the Spaniards. In 1680, they rose up and drove the Spanish out of New Mexico. But the victory only lasted 12 years. As the Spanish returned, some Pueblo bands migrated into Dinétah.

Raiding

Raiding by Navajo riders angered the Spanish. They considered it theft. The idea behind raiding, however, was more complicated. The Navajo, like many native peoples, had raided their rivals long before Europeans arrived. Warriors did this not just to acquire goods, but to earn respect for their daring and bravery. Because being captured might mean torture and death, a warrior considered raided goods a fair and legal reward for taking risks.

The Navajo captured 20,000 mules and horses and 800,000 sheep and cattle in raids over a period of four years in the 1800s.

On Guard

During this troubled time, the Navajo built towers of stone and wood around the rims of mesas. These **pueblitos** helped the Navajo in two ways. First, a pueblito's location gave watchers a view of the land below. Second, the Navajo put up pueblitos in places good for cutting off attackers. Often, one pueblito could be seen from another. Navajos could then send a warning from tower to tower when enemies approached.

This pueblito was built on a large boulder.

Simon Canyon Ruin is a Navajo pueblito that dates back to 1754.

Many Navajo raised both goats and sheep. Both animals were sources of milk, meat, and wool.

For the most part the Navajo and Spanish kept peace during the 1700s. But other Indian peoples such as the Comanche rode in from the Great Plains to raid the Navajo and their Apache cousins. By then, the Navajo were raiding less. Instead, they mostly farmed and hunted. They also turned to raising livestock, especially sheep. Raids for sheep, cows, and horses, however, would bring clashes with powerful new enemies.

Seven hundred U.S. soldiers and more than twice as many Mexican troops lost their lives in the Battle of Buena Vista during the Mexican-American War.

CHAPTER 3

The Navajo's Conflicts

Mexico gained its **independence** from Spain in 1821. For the next 25 years, Mexicans and Navajos fought one another, raiding, attacking, and taking prisoners. In 1846, Mexico went to war with the United States. In the Mexican-American War, U.S. soldiers tried to take over New Mexico (then part of Mexico), including Navajo territory. The war ended with the United States claiming land in and around Dinétah.

The Mexican-American War is known in Mexico as the American Invasion of Mexico.

When many soldiers left the Southwest to fight in the Civil War, the Navajo mistakenly believed their efforts against the military were working.

Treaties and Trouble

After the United States defeated Mexico, the governor of the New Mexico Territory made a **treaty** with some Navajo leaders. The treaty gave the United States permission to build forts in Dinétah. Traders followed the U.S. Army and set up businesses. Navajos who did not agree with the treaty raided the traders as well as white settlers' livestock. The U.S. Army failed to stop them. Then, in 1861, the soldiers went east to fight in the U.S. Civil War. Navajos could then raid without fear.

The Final Clash

As the raids worsened, New Mexico's settlers formed a **militia** to attack the Navajo and take prisoners. General James H. Carleton ordered famed explorer Kit Carson to go to Dinétah to bring the Navajo to a reservation—land set aside for them to live on. Carson was joined by New Mexicans looking for revenge. From late 1863 into 1864, Carson's men destroyed Navajo crops, slaughtered their livestock, and burned their homes.

By destroying crops and animals, Carson and his men left the Navajo without food for the winter.

To the Navajo, Carson was known as Red Clothes because of his red underwear.

Defeat and Removal

In January 1864, Carson and the militia battled the Navajo at Canyon de Chelly. Twenty-three Navajo died. More than 200 gave up. The remaining Navajo, having lost their crops and animals, faced starvation. They had no choice but to surrender. Beginning in early 1864, the U.S. Army led about 8,000 Navajo men, women, and children out of Dinétah on what became known as the Long Walk.

In 1863, many Navajo tried to hide from Carson in Canyon de Chelly. There, many starved or were shot by soldiers.

Pregnant women who went into labor on the journey were killed.

Only very old, young, or sick Navajo rode in wagons during the Long Walk. The rest were forced to walk.

The Long Walk

The army marched the Navajo over more than 450 miles (725 kilometers) of land. During the 18-day march, the Navajo prisoners coped with too little firewood, no fresh water, and either bitter cold or blazing heat. A number of people died crossing the Rio Grande. Those unable to keep up were shot by soldiers. An unknown number—maybe hundreds—died on the way.

Land of Suffering

The Long Walk was not a single event. The Navajo were marched in groups. Some made the trip during the heat of summer, and others through the snow of winter.

The Long Walk ended at the Bosque Redondo Reservation, a place the Navajo called Hweeldi, "the place of suffering." Located on 40 square miles (100 sq km) of land, Bosque Redondo was laid out for only 5,000 people , but 8,000 were forced to live there. In 1868, after years of Navajo hardship, the army admitted its reservation idea had failed. A new treaty allowed the Navajo to return to Dinétah. By then, however, more than 2,300 people had died.

Disease

Crowding sick and exhausted people together allowed deadly diseases such as pneumonia and smallpox to spread. The Navajo had no immunity to European illnesses like smallpox, and they died in great numbers.

Poor Housing

Unable to build their usual houses, the Navajo had to make shelters out of sticks, canvas, and other materials. The shelters failed to protect people from heat or cold. The Navajo were also forced to build brick housing for U.S. troops.

Caterpillars called cutworms destroyed the corn crops that managed to grow.

Lack of Water

Desert farmers had to store water to use on crops during the hot summers. At Bosque Redondo, however, the water system failed. The broken system, combined with drought, left the Navajo unable to grow food.

Fort Defiance was created in an effort to control the Navajo. It eventually served as an agency for the Navajo Reservation.

CHAPTER 4

The Navajo Nation

The Navajo and their neighbors continued to fight after the return to Dinétah. To keep the trouble under control, the U.S. Army maintained its forts within the Navajo homeland. Other Navajo land was soon taken for other reasons. Railroads seized pieces of it to lay tracks. Miners dug up other places. Though the Navajo were promised payment for the land, they often received nothing.

 Fort Defiance was abandoned as a military post in the 1860s.

Lack of Rights

The Navajo lived on their **sacred** land, but they had no rights. Often, outsiders attacked them or accused them of crimes they did not commit. If a Navajo was blamed for stealing horses, whites might murder him and get away with it. Soldiers hired Navajo scouts to gather information on other Navajos' plans against whites when whites and Navajos clashed. U.S. Army officers believed Navajos were more likely to trust another Navajo than a white soldier.

Navajo scouts

Many Navajo parents blocked the entrance to their homes to keep officials from taking their children to school.

Attacking Navajo Ways

After 1868, the United States tried to erase Navajo culture. Many Navajo resisted sending their children to U.S. schools. The Navajo schoolchildren were forced to speak English and punished for using their native language. But the government plan to extinguish the Navajo language didn't work. Today, most Navajos do speak English. But almost all also speak Diné Bizaad, the native Navajo language.

The Navajo made some dyes for wool thread from roots, flowers, and berries.

Navajo girls learn to weave from their mothers, aunts, and grandmothers.

The Sheep Slaughter

Between 1868 and the 1930s, the sheep population in Dinétah boomed to more than 500,000. The Navajo took advantage of this and made beautiful rugs from the wool. Sales from the rugs made them money. Because more sheep meant more wool, keeping large sheep herds helped improve their quality of life. But in the 1930s, U.S. government officials said that all those sheep harmed the land by grazing too much.

The government announced it would limit the number of livestock the Navajo could have. When the Navajo refused to get rid of their sheep, government officials killed four out of every five of the animals. The slaughter all but ruined Navajo sheep ranching and rug making for a time. The Navajo suffered additional harm beginning in 1944, when companies dumped poisonous waste from **uranium** mines on Navajo lands. Uranium waste causes cancer and other serious health problems.

A Navajo herds sheep. In the 1930s, U.S. government officials shot Navajo sheep and left them to rot.

Modern Times

During the 20th century, the Navajo slowly bounced back and became the Navajo Nation. The nation's land expanded to about 27,000 square miles (70,000 sq km). Inside its borders today, the Navajo elect their own government, raise their own flag, and keep their own police force. They earn money from coal and oil mining, tourism, and selling arts and crafts. Today, more than 250,000 people live in the Navajo Nation.

The rainbow represents the Navajo right to self-government.

The Navajo flag features an outline of Navajo homelands and the tribal seal, surrounded by four mountains.

When the United States entered World War II, the U.S. Marines realized they needed a code language the enemy could not understand. Diné Bizaad, the Navajo language, was perfect. It was a spoken rather than written language. It was also very complicated and hard to learn. In fact, it had almost no speakers outside the Navajo Nation. Navajo marines invented a code and later used it to send messages during important battles at Iwo Jima and elsewhere.

Code talkers used Navajo words for animals to represent certain objects or ideas. For example, the code word for *battleship* was the Navajo term for *whale*.

One hogan often housed
not only parents and
children, but also
grandparents and other
family members.

CHAPTER 5

Navajo Culture

Before modern times, the traditional Navajo dwelling was a dome-shaped building called a hogan. Navajos built a hogan by covering a frame of wood with clay, stone, more wood, or other materials. They always placed the hogan's door facing east to welcome the morning sun. According to Navajo stories, the hero Coyote learned hogan building from the Beaver People. He then built a hogan for the First Man and First Woman.

← Hogans did not have windows.

The Hogan in Everyday Life

The hogan was an important part of Navajo life. The Navajo believed a lonely spirit dwelt inside. To give it attention, they sang sacred songs. Otherwise, the lonely hogan might attract evil spirits. A family could not move into a hogan until a medicine man blessed the structure. The Navajo thought of hogans as male or female. Important ceremonies took place in special five-sided male hogans. Families lived in female hogans.

Timeline of Navajo History

1539
The Spanish arrive in the Southwest.

1864
The Navajo are forced on the Long Walk to Bosque Redondo.

The Medicine Man

In Navajo culture, a medicine man led sacred ceremonies. A medicine man's difficult training could take more than 20 years to complete. During his training, he mastered hundreds of **rituals**, for as many occasions. The rituals revolved around sandpainting. A medicine man used colored sand and minerals to make a sandpainting's complicated design. The Navajo believed each sandpainting was a being that lived in both the spirit world and our world.

1868
The Navajo return to Dinétah.

1930s
Navajo sheep are slaughtered by the U.S. government.

A medicine man might use a sandpainting to heal others. For example, he chanted as his sick patient sat on the sandpainting. The Navajo believed that spirits then came into the world through the sandpainting and took away the illness. The sandpainting then had to be destroyed. For that reason, a sandpainting, no matter how beautiful, remained in place for no more than a day. Later on, the Navajo forbade anyone to photograph a sandpainting, to protect its sacred power.

The dried blossoms of certain flowers, such as larkspur delphinium, were used to create shades of blue for sandpaintings.

Arts and Crafts

Navajo culture also valued the creation of permanent artwork. That remains true today. Like the Pueblo peoples, the Navajo make **kachina** dolls. Unlike the Pueblo dolls, however, Navajo kachinas have no religious purpose. They are simply a craft. In addition, the Navajo are world famous for weaving wool into rugs. While the Navajo may weave for art or money, they also consider weaving an opportunity to get together with friends and family.

The most valuable kachinas are made from a single piece of root from the cottonwood tree.

Navajo tradition holds that the spirit Spider Woman first taught the Navajo to weave.

Some rugs have geometric shapes. Others include figures of people or animals from stories or everyday life.

The simple rug patterns reflect the Navajo view that the world is balanced and organized. In fact, Navajo tradition says the world itself is woven together. Navajo patterns appeal to non-Navajo, too. Navajo rugs hang in museums and earn money for today's weavers.

Modern Navajo jewelry makers work silver into earrings, hairpins, bracelets, and buckles for use by Navajos and non-Navajos alike. Art, like history and religious belief, weaves together the Navajo's past and present. ★

True Statistics

Time the Diné first traded with Pueblo peoples: 1200s

Time needed to study to become a medicine man: More than 20 years

Time it took to make the Long Walk: 18 days

Number of people who made the Long Walk: About 8,000

Number of sheep owned by Navajo in 1930: More than 500,000

Percentage of Navajo-owned sheep lost between 1934 and 1952 because of government slaughter: 80

Number of Navajo code talkers during World War II: 29

Area of Navajo Nation today: 27,000 sq. mi. (70,000 sq km)

Population of the Navajo Nation today: 250,000

Did you find the truth?

(T) In the 1930s, the U.S. government killed more than four-fifths of the livestock on Navajo lands.

(F) Kachina dolls are sacred objects to the Navajo.

Resources

Books

Birchfield, D. L. *Navajo*. New York: Gareth Stevens, 2003.

Bruchac, Joseph. *Navajo Long Walk*. Des Moines, IA: National Geographic Children's Books, 2002.

Craats, Rennay. *The Navajo*. New York: Chelsea House, 2004.

King, David C. *The Navajo*. New York: Benchmark, 2006.

Lassieur, Allison. *The Navajo: A Proud People*. Berkeley Heights, NJ: Enslow, 2005.

Santella, Andrew. *Navajo Code Talkers*. Minneapolis: Compass Point, 2004.

Sonneborn, Liz. *The Navajos*. Minneapolis: Lerner Classroom, 2007.

Woods, Geraldine. *The Navajo*. Danbury, CT: Franklin Watts, 2002.

Organizations and Web Sites

Navajo Nation
www.navajo.org/history.htm
Find out about Navajo history and link to news about what's going on today in the Navajo Nation.

Smithsonian National Museum of the American Indian: Native Words, Native Warriors
www.nmai.si.edu/education/codetalkers
Learn the complete story of the Native American code talkers through photographs, biographies, and code details.

Places to Visit

National Museum of the American Indian
Fourth Street & Independence Ave., SW
Washington, DC 20560
(202) 633-1000
www.nmai.si.edu
View exhibits on the lives and cultures of Native Americans.

Navajo Nation Museum
Highway 264 and Loop Road
P.O. Box 1840
Window Rock, AZ 86515
(928) 871-7941
www.navajonationmuseum.org
See exhibits devoted to Navajo art and history.

Important Words

Athabascan (a-tha-BAS-kin)—the family of Native American languages that includes Navajo

drought (DROUT)—a long period of unusually low rainfall

independence (in-di-PEN-duhnss)—a state of not being controlled by others

kachina (ka-CHEEN-a)—a wooden doll that represents a god or a spirit of an ancestor

mesas (MAY-suhzz)—broad, flat-topped hills with steep sides

migrated (MYE-grate-ed)—moved from one place to another

militia (muh-LISH-uh)—people called up in an emergency to act as soldiers

pueblitos (pwe-BLEE-tows)—small towers made of stone or wood, built by the Navajo

rituals (RICH-oo-ulz)—religious ceremonies with specific rules

sacred (SAY-krid)—related to religion or something holy

traditional (treh-DISH-uhn-ul)—established patterns of thought or action passed down from generation to generation

treaty (TREE-tee)—an agreement or deal that is legally binding on the two or more groups who sign

uranium (yu-RAY-nee-uhm)—a metal used in nuclear weapons

Index

Page numbers in **bold** indicate illustrations

ancestors, 7
Apache people, 14, 16, 19
artwork, **32**, 33, 39–**40**, 41–**42**
Athabascan language, 7, 14

Bosque Redondo Reservation, 26, **27**, 31, 38

Carson, Kit, **23**, 24
Catholicism, 13
children, 24, **31**, **36**
clothing, 9
code talkers, **35**
Comanche people, 19

Diné people, 7, 8, 9, 10, 13
Dinétah territory, 10–**11**, 13, 16, 21, 22, 23, 24, 26, 29, 32, **39**
diseases, 27
drought, 16, 27

education, **31**
European exploration, 11, **12**, 15, **38**

families, **36**, 38, 41
farming, 9, 15, 19, 23, 24, 27
food, 8, **9**, 16, 24, 27
forts, 14, 22, **28**, 29
Four Corners region, **10**, **11**

hogans (houses), **36**, 37, 38
horses, **15**–16, **17**, 19, 30
houses, 23, 27, **36**, 37, 38
hunting, 8, 9, 19

kachina dolls, **41**

languages, 7, 14, 31, 35
livestock, **14**, **17**, **19**, 22, 23, 24, 32–**33**, **39**

Long Walk, 24, **25**, **26**–**27**, **38**

map, **6**
medicine men, 38, 39–40
mesas, **10**, 18
Mexican-American War, **20**, 21
Mexico, 13, **20**, 21, 22
mining, 13, 29, 33, 34
Monument Valley, **10**

Navajo Nation, 34

population, 34
pottery, **8**
pueblitos, **18**
Pueblo peoples, **8**, **9**, **12**, 13, **14**, **16**, 41

raids, **14**, 16, **17**, 19, 21, 22, 23
religions, 10, 13, 37, 38, 39–40
reservations, 23, 26, **28**
rituals, 39

sandpaintings, 39–**40**
settlers, 15, 22, 23
Spain, 11, **12**, 13–14, 15, **16**, 17, 19, 21, **38**

territory, **6**, 10–**11**, 13, 16, 21, 22, 23, 24, 26, 29, 32, **34**, **39**
timeline, **38**–**39**
tools, **9**
trade, 8, 9, 22
treaties, 22, 26

U.S. Army, **20**, **22**, 24, 25, 26, 27, 29, 30
U.S. Marines, **35**

war, 15, **16**, **20**, 21, **22**, 24, 30, **35**
weaving, **32**, 33, 41–**42**
women, **8**, 24, 25, 38

About the Authors

Kevin Cunningham has written more than 40 books on disasters, the history of disease, Native Americans, and other topics. Cunningham lives near Chicago with his wife and young daughter.

Peter Benoit is educated as a mathematician but has many other interests. He has taught and tutored high school and college students for many years, mostly in math and science. He also runs summer workshops for writers and students of literature. Benoit has written more than 2,000 poems. His life has been one committed to learning. He lives in Greenwich, New York.